NORWAY

Deborah Kopka

Lerner Publications Company • Minneapolis

Lerner Publications Company
A division of Lerner Publishing Group, Inc.
241 First Avenue North
Minneapolis, MN 55401 U.S.A.

Website address: www.lernerbooks.com

Library of Congress Cataloging-in-Publication Data

Kopka, Deborah L.
       Norway / by Deborah Kopka.
          p.   cm. — (Country explorers)
       Includes index.
       ISBN 978–1–58013–603–7 (lib. bdg. : alk. paper)
       1. Norway—Juvenile literature. I. Title.
    DL409.K67 2010
    948.1—dc22   2009019481

Manufactured in the United States of America
1 – VI – 12/15/09

Table of Contents

Welcome!

We're going to Norway! Norwegians call their country Norge. The word means the "way to the North." It is easy to see why! On the continent of Europe, Norway is the country farthest to the north.

Norway curves over the top of Finland to meet Russia. Sweden touches eastern Norway. The Norwegian Sea lies to the west. The North Sea spreads across the south. Skagerrak is an arm of the North Sea.

ARCTIC CIRCLE

The city of Alesund is built on seven islands in the Norwegian Sea.

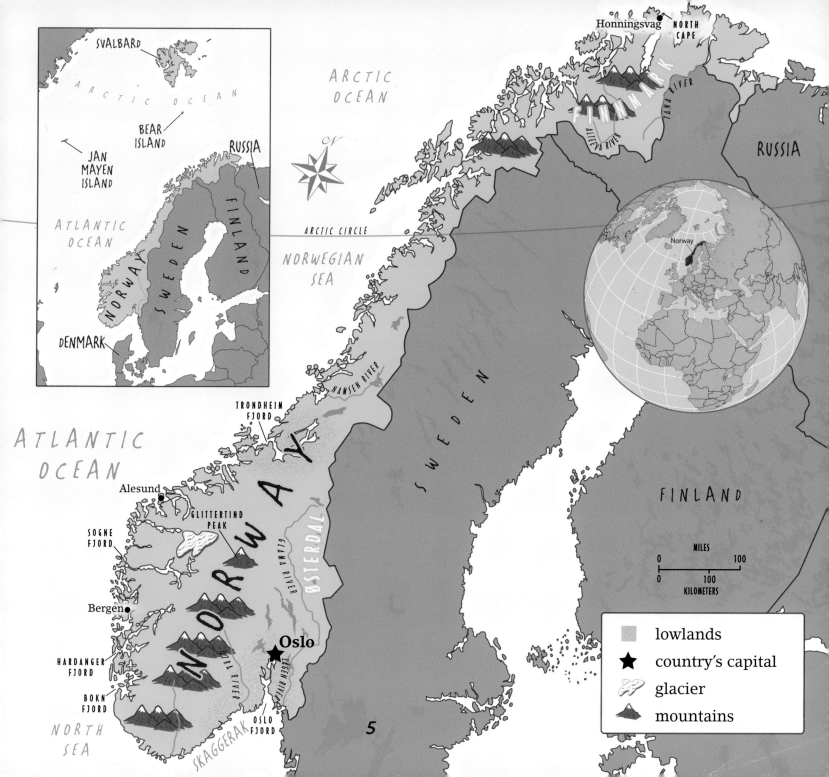

SVALBARD

ARCTIC OCEAN

BEAR ISLAND

JAN MAYEN ISLAND

RUSSIA

ATLANTIC OCEAN

NORWAY

SWEDEN

FINLAND

DENMARK

Honningsvag

NORTH CAPE

ARCTIC OCEAN

FINNMARK

ALTEVA RIVER

TANA RIVER

RUSSIA

ARCTIC CIRCLE

NORWEGIAN SEA

Norway

ATLANTIC OCEAN

NAMSEN RIVER

TRONDHEIM FJORD

S W E D E N

Alesund

GLITTERTIND PEAK

SOGNE FJORD

N O R W A Y

OSTERDAL

GLAMA RIVER

FINLAND

MILES
0   100

0   100
KILOMETERS

Bergen

HARDANGER FJORD

OTRA RIVER

LAGEN RIVER

Oslo

BOKN FJORD

OSLO FJORD

NORTH SEA

SKAGGERAK

5

	lowlands
★	country's capital
	glacier
	mountains

Mountains and Fjords

Norway has many mountain ranges. They are in the north and the south. Deep valleys separate the mountains. Some valleys have forested slopes. Others have rocky slopes. High in the mountains are huge ice fields called glaciers.

A small town sits at the base of a mountain in northern Norway.

The mountains slant into the sea in western Norway. Deep bays, called fjords, lead from the sea into the countryside. Norway's fjords make the coastline zigzag.

A cruise ship sails through a deep fjord.

Heading Downhill

Most Norwegians live in southeastern Norway. In the east, the Osterdal is Norway's longest valley. Thick forests carpet it.

Trees cover the sides of the Osterdal in southeastern Norway.

Keep heading south! You will hit Oslo. That's the capital of Norway. Forests and lakes cover most of Oslo.

Map Whiz Quiz

Check out the map on page 5. Trace an outline of the map onto a piece of paper. Find the Norwegian Sea. Mark it with a *W* for west. Next, find Sweden. Mark it with an *E* for east. Trace the line of the Arctic Circle that goes around the North Pole. Put an N for north above the Arctic Circle. Look for the North Sea. Mark it with an *S* for south.

The city of Oslo curves around the edge of the Oslo Fjord.

Finnmark

The Arctic Circle cuts through Norway. This imaginary line marks a circle around the North Pole. That is the world's most northern point. Finnmark is the part of Norway that lies farthest north. It is high in the Arctic Circle. In Finnmark, the sun shines day and night for ten whole weeks in summer. In winter, it stays dark for about that long.

Snow covers the land along the seacoast in Finnmark.

The sun shines at midnight on North Cape, a steep cliff on the northern edge of Finnmark.

11

How's the Weather?

Most of Norway has a mild climate. Summer temperatures range between 60 and 72°F (15 and 22°C). Winter temperatures on the coasts do not drop far below 25°F (-4°C). But it is colder in northern and eastern Norway. When winter snows fall, Norwegians do not mind. They happily get out their skis!

Hikers enjoy the view in a sunny Norwegian valley.

Skis are the perfect way to travel over the snow during a Norwegian winter.

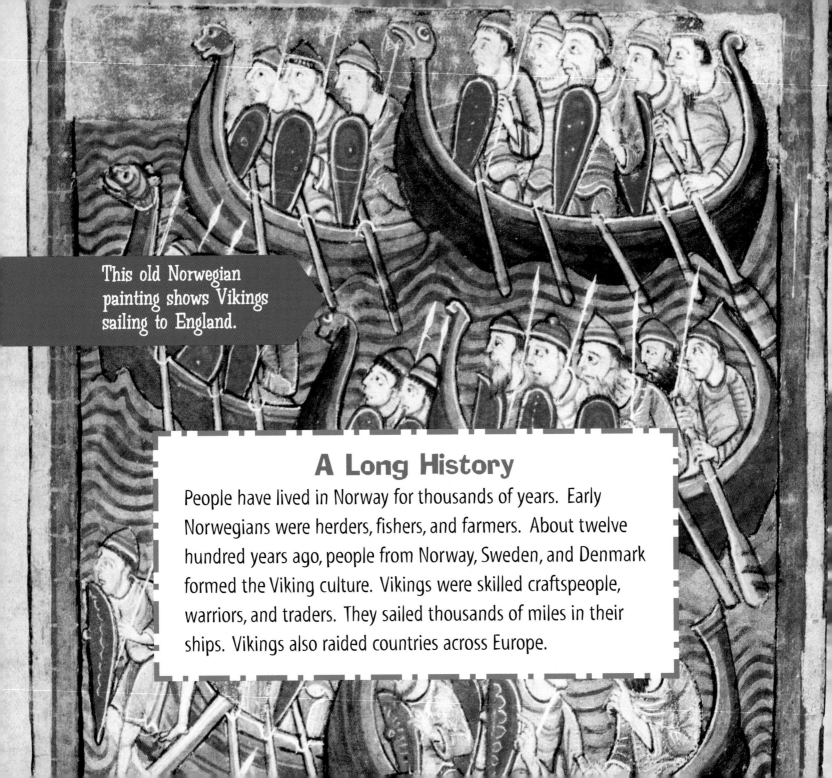

This old Norwegian painting shows Vikings sailing to England.

A Long History

People have lived in Norway for thousands of years. Early Norwegians were herders, fishers, and farmers. About twelve hundred years ago, people from Norway, Sweden, and Denmark formed the Viking culture. Vikings were skilled craftspeople, warriors, and traders. They sailed thousands of miles in their ships. Vikings also raided countries across Europe.

From 1030 to 1380, Norway was its own country. Between 1380 and 1814, Norway was part of Denmark. (Denmark is south of Norway.) Then, in 1814, Norway united with Sweden. Finally, in 1905, Norway became its own nation again.

Norway still has a royal family. This picture shows Queen Sonja and King Harald V (*center*) with their children and grandchildren in 2006.

The Norwegians

In each part of Norway, people have a different *bunad*, or national costume. Norwegians may wear their bunads at special times, such as holidays.

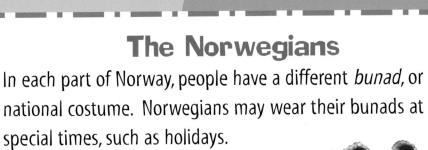

Two children wear their bunads during a holiday celebration.

Many Norwegians have blond hair and blue eyes. Others have brown hair or brown eyes. People from Asia, Africa, North America, and South America also live in Norway.

A Norwegian family warms up on a cool summer day.

17

The Sami

About forty thousand members of the Sami ethnic group live in Norway. Finnmark is their age-old home. The Sami came from central Asia thousands of years ago. They may have been Norway's first people.

A Sami family stands in front of a typical house, which is called a *lavvu*.

The Sami used to follow herds of reindeer. But many modern Sami work as farmers, loggers, or fishers. Most Sami kids live, dress, and go to school like other Norwegian kids. Some Sami wear old-fashioned clothes every day. But most Sami wear them only at special times.

A Sami man watches his reindeer herd.

19

Let's Eat

Many Norwegians like to eat big breakfasts. They might include cereal, meat, herring, cheese, and buttered bread with jam. At lunchtime, workers and kids pull out a tasty *smorbrod* brought from home. Smorbrods are special sandwiches. They're made without the top layer of bread. In the evening, people eat filling dinners. Soup, meat or fish, potatoes, vegetables, and dessert might be served.

A Norwegian family enjoys an outdoor breakfast.

At special times, Norwegians have buffet meals. At a buffet, tables are covered with platters piled high with food. People choose what they like. Meat, seafood, vegetables, cheeses, thin bread, and desserts are among the choices.

Norway

Dear Penny:
Norway is cool! Dad rented a boat today. He steered us around little islands that poke out of the ocean. We ate tasty smorbrods. The day was a lot of fun.

Wish you were here!

Lucy

Your F
Your
Anywh

Bokmal or Nynorsk?

The Norwegian language is spoken and written in two ways. Bokmal is standard Norwegian. Nynorsk is new Norwegian. They sound almost alike. Outside major cities, you'll hear many local Norwegian dialects, or ways of speaking. Norwegians can understand Bokmal, Nynorsk, and local dialects. But Norwegians cannot understand the Sami language unless they have learned it.

Most magazines and newspapers are written in Bokmal.

UNIVERSITETSSYKEHUSET NORD-NORGE HF
DAVVI-NORGGA UNIVERSITEHTABUOHCCEVIESSU

Hovedinngang

Váldouksa

The sign at this hospital in Tromso is written in Bokmal first and then in Sami.

School

Norwegian children start first grade when they turn seven. Students in grades one through six don't get grades. But they still have to study! Their teachers send home reports twice a year. Twice a year, teachers grade students in grades seven through nine.

Children play outside a school in northern Norway.

Students study Norwegian, religion, math, English, social studies, and music in grades four, five, and six. All students study Sami history and culture.

Small Schools

Many Norwegian children live in tiny villages. Small schools are scattered across the countryside. Of the 3,000 schools in Norway, 650 have fewer than thirty students.

Students at a school in Finnmark learn the Sami language.

Kids

Many Norwegian parents work outside the home. When no parent is at home, a *dogmamma* looks after young children. A dogmamma is usually a family friend or a neighbor.

These two mothers take turns taking care of each other's children.

All in the Family

Here are the Norwegian words for family members. Practice using these terms on your own family. See if they understand you.

grandfather	bestefar	(BEHS-tuh-fahr)
grandmother	bestemor	(BEHS-tuh-moor)
father	far	(FAHR)
mother	mor	(MOOR)
uncle	onkel	(OHNG-kuhl)
aunt	tante	(TUHN-tuh)
brother	bror	(BROOR)
sister	soster	(SOOHR-stuhr)

Two children take a boat tour of a fjord with their grandparents.

Colorful houses line a street in the northern town of Honningsvag

Buildings

Cozy, brightly painted houses dot Norway's countryside. Homes are tucked into valleys. Some homes overlook lakes and fjords. City dwellers might rent apartments in large buildings.

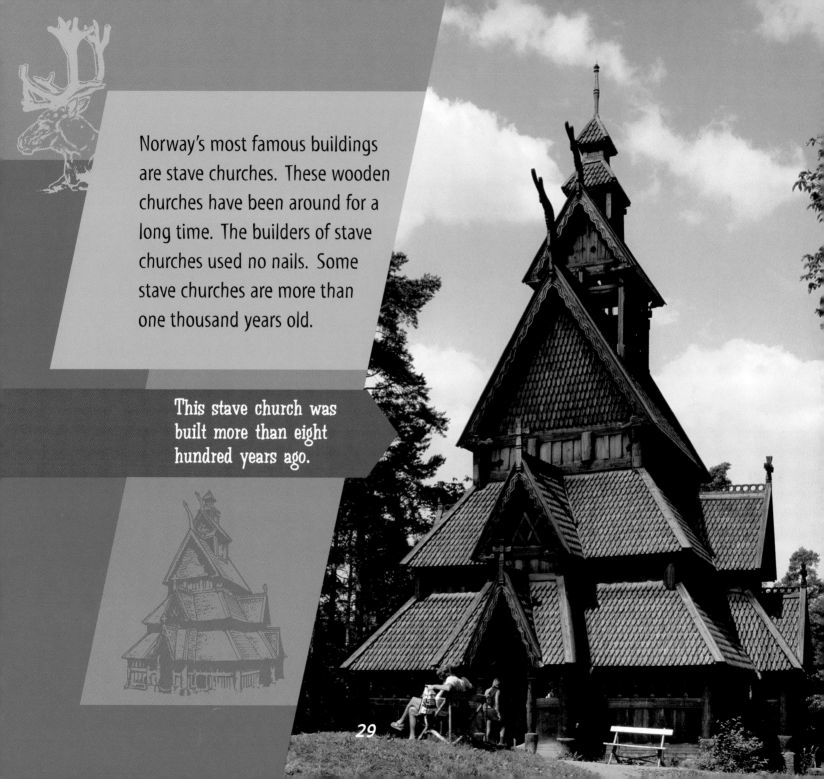

Norway's most famous buildings are stave churches. These wooden churches have been around for a long time. The builders of stave churches used no nails. Some stave churches are more than one thousand years old.

This stave church was built more than eight hundred years ago.

Hit the Slopes!

Norwegian children are said to be "born with skis on their feet." Kids start skiing at the age of two or three. They learn how to skate and sled too.

A three-year-old crosses a snowy Norwegian field on skis.

Norwegians like to be outdoors in the summertime. Folks fish in fjords, lakes, and streams. Boats zip around Norway's coasts. Many Norwegians enjoy hiking in the country's national forests.

A Norwegian family hikes in the mountains.

Keep the Beat!

Most Norwegians love music. Students learn to play a musical instrument. They may play the violin, the trumpet, or the flute. Many kids take part in school bands.

A girl practices her flute at home in Oslo.

Children and adults enjoy jazz and rock music. On the radio, they hear the songs of favorite Norwegian pop groups, such as Royksopp and Madrugada.

Edvard Grieg

Edvard Grieg (1843–1907) is one of the greatest music writers of all time. He often used music from Norwegian folk tunes. In modern times, music lovers still honor Grieg.

Edvard Grieg wrote many famous pieces of music.

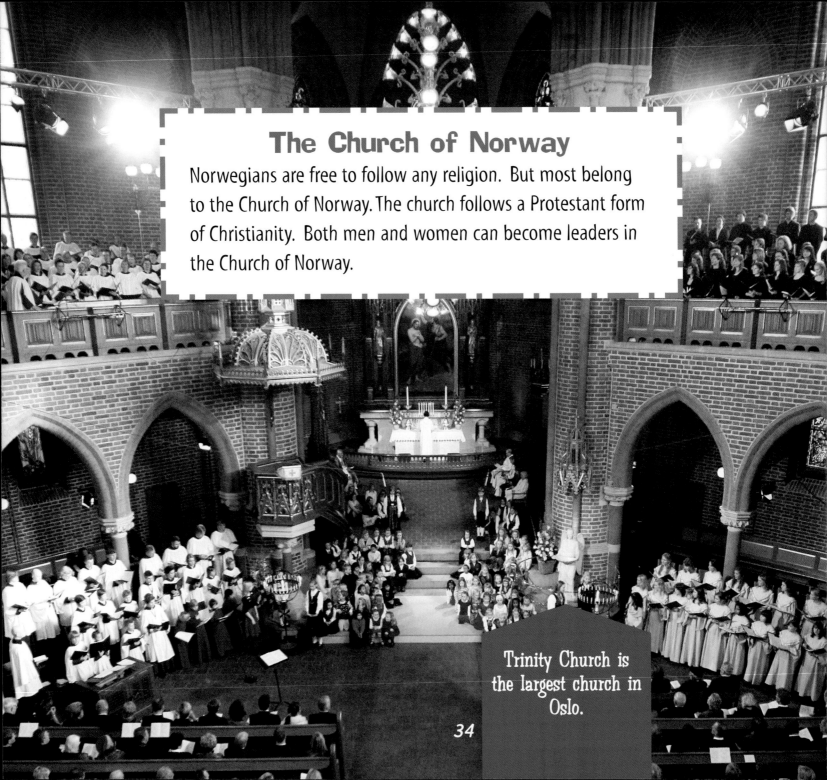

The Church of Norway

Norwegians are free to follow any religion. But most belong to the Church of Norway. The church follows a Protestant form of Christianity. Both men and women can become leaders in the Church of Norway.

Trinity Church is the largest church in Oslo.

A baby joins the Church of Norway through baptism.
After the baptism, guests attend a fancy lunch. The baby
gets gifts, such as a first Bible.

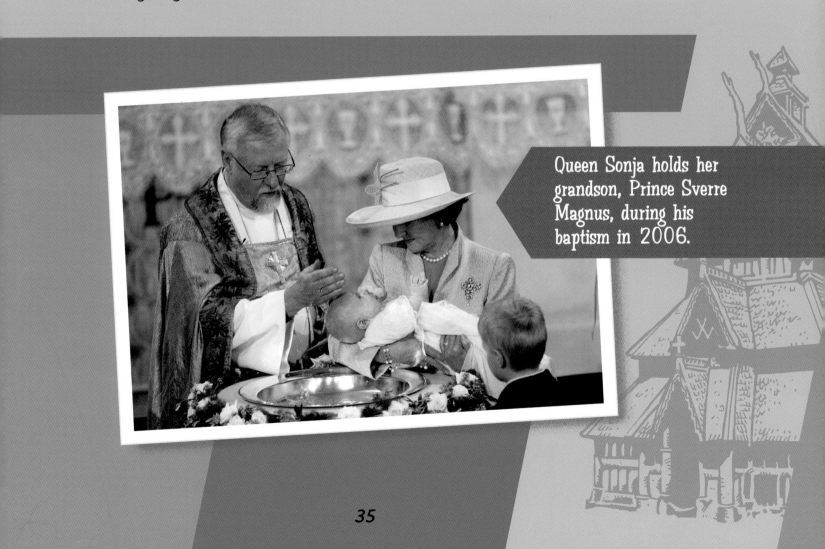

Queen Sonja holds her grandson, Prince Sverre Magnus, during his baptism in 2006.

Celebrating Holidays

On June 23, Norwegians celebrate Midsummer Night. That is the longest day of the year. People light huge bonfires. Norwegians honor the day with singing, dancing, and feasting.

On Christmas Eve (December 24), most Norwegians go to church. Afterward, families gather for a big meal. Save room for cookies and treats! And don't forget the tower cake, called *kransekake*. After eating dinner, folks gather around a Christmas tree to open gifts.

This kransekake has been decorated with Norwegian flags.

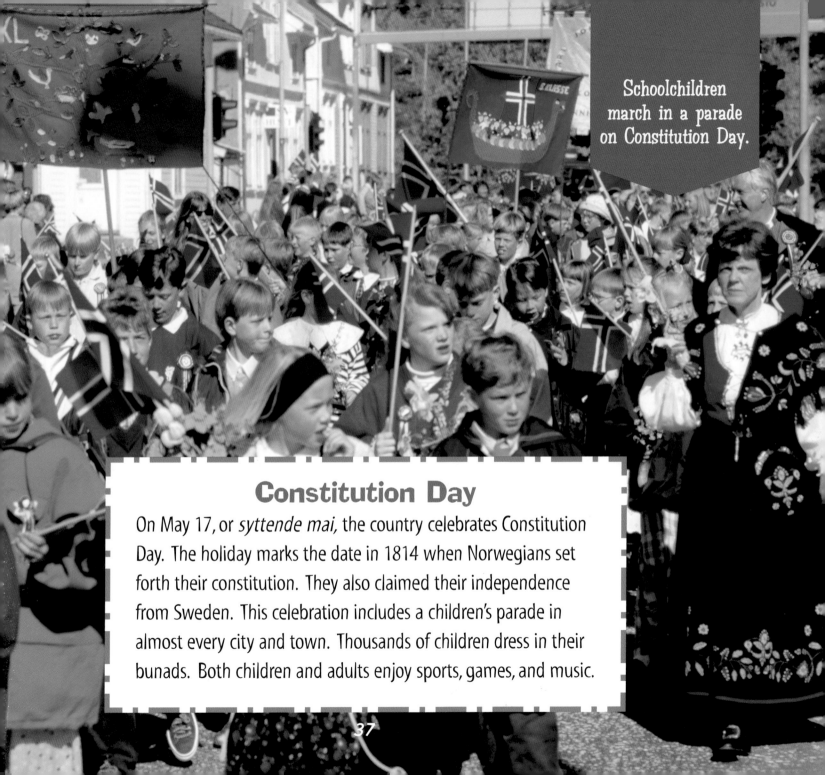

Schoolchildren march in a parade on Constitution Day.

Constitution Day

On May 17, or *syttende mai,* the country celebrates Constitution Day. The holiday marks the date in 1814 when Norwegians set forth their constitution. They also claimed their independence from Sweden. This celebration includes a children's parade in almost every city and town. Thousands of children dress in their bunads. Both children and adults enjoy sports, games, and music.

Made by Hand

Norwegians can head to the store to buy what they need. But many choose to make things themselves. They might carve wooden furniture or weave rugs. Some knit fancy sweaters with beautiful snowflake patterns. Many Norwegians have handmade bunads.

A couple tries on Norwegian sweaters decorated with snowflakes.

Make a Clove Ball!

Many Norwegian kids like to make crafts at Christmastime. Here's a favorite! The spicy scent will last long after the orange has dried out.

You will need:
1 large fresh navel orange
1 cup of whole cloves

1. Wash the orange with a damp kitchen towel. Allow the orange to sit at room temperature for one hour.
2. Gently push the cloves into the orange, one at a time. Work on one small area. Then move to the next one and the next until you have covered the entire orange.
3. Tie a bright ribbon around the orange.

Cloved oranges can make your room smell wonderful!

39

Grab a Book!

Norwegians love to curl up with a book. Lots of people choose exciting best sellers. Many also pick books from Norway's past.

A family reads together on a chilly winter night.

In the late 1800s, some Norwegians became famous writers. Bjornstjerne Bjornson wrote stories, novels, poetry, and plays. He also wrote the words to the Norwegian national song.

Sigrid Undset wrote *Kristin Lavransdatter.* This book is about a Norwegian girl who lived long ago. Norway's most famous playwright is Henrik Ibsen. He wrote twenty-five plays. Several are still being performed in many countries.

Sigrid Undset reads from *Kristin Lavransdatter.*

Story Time

"Once upon a time" starts lots of Norwegian folktales. Families passed down the stories through the years. The stories often teach a lesson about life. Other tales tell of people or talking animals who outsmart dangerous creatures.

Children listen to a storyteller in this Norwegian painting from 1844.

Three Billy Goats Gruff

Once upon a time, a small goat skipped over a bridge leading to a grassy meadow. But a troll living under the bridge wanted to eat the goat. The goat begged the troll to wait. A bigger goat would be a better meal! So the troll let the little goat pass to the grassy meadow. Soon a medium-size goat trotted along the bridge. The goat told the troll to wait to eat his even bigger brother. The troll agreed. Soon a huge goat with giant horns thundered across the bridge. The troll jumped onto the bridge, ready for his feast. But the large goat used his horns to toss the troll off the bridge. Then the goat joined his brothers in the meadow.

Trolls appear in many Norwegian stories. Some trolls are big and dangerous. Others are small and tricky.

THE FLAG OF NORWAY

Norway's flag has a red background with a blue and white cross. The colors stand for revolution and liberty. The flag was created in 1821.

FAST FACTS

FULL COUNTRY NAME: The Kingdom of Norway

AREA: 125,050 square miles (323,878 square kilometers), a little larger than the state of New Mexico

MAIN LANDFORMS: the mountain ranges Dovrefjell, Jotunheimen, Kjolen, and Langfjella; the lowlands; the fjords Bokn, Hardanger, Oslo, Sogne, and Trondheim; glaciers; valleys; rolling hills; peninsulas.

MAJOR RIVERS: Alteelva, Glama, Lagen, Namsen, Orkla, Otra, and Tana

ANIMALS AND THEIR HABITATS: bears, elk, ferrets, foxes, reindeer, wolves (forests); beavers, fish, otters (streams); puffins, whales (ocean)

CAPITAL CITY: Oslo

OFFICIAL LANGUAGE: Norwegian

POPULATION: about 4,644,500

GLOSSARY

baptism: a Christian ceremony that brings people into the religion

capital: a city where the government of a state or country is located

continent: one of seven large areas of land. The continents are Africa, Antarctica, Asia, Australia, Europe, North America, and South America.

dialect: a local language that sounds different from other versions of the same language

ethnic group: a group of people with many things in common, such as language, religion, and customs

fjord: a narrow water channel from the ocean. Steep cliffs often surround fjords.

folktale: a timeless story told by word of mouth from grandparent to parent to child. Many folktales have been written down in books.

glacier: a huge sheet of ice that moves slowly over land

map: a drawing or chart of all or part of Earth or the sky

Vikings: a people who lived in Norway, Denmark, and Sweden long ago. They traveled to many faraway lands.

TO LEARN MORE

BOOKS

Haig, Matt. *Samuel Blink and the Forbidden Forest.* New York: Penguin Group, 2008. Two children wander into a bewitched forest in Norway where they meet characters from Norwegian folklore.

Knudsen, Shannon. *Giants, Trolls, and Ogres.* Minneapolis: Lerner Publications Company, 2010. Explore the folklore of these fantastical creatures and their connections to history and culture.

Landau, Elaine. *Norway.* Danbury, CT: Children's Press, 2000. Learn about Norway's geography in this informative book.

Limke, Jeff. *Thor & Loki: In the Land of Giants.* Minneapolis: Graphic Universe, 2007. Read the stories of Thor and Loki, two of the most famous gods of Norse mythology.

WEBSITES

National Geographic Kids
http://magma.nationalgeographic.com/ngexplorer/0511/articles/mainarticle.html
View a Viking house, ship, and a mystery map, and learn about Viking village life, explorations, and attacks.

Roald Amundsen (1872–1928)
http://www.south-pole.com/p0000101.htm
Find out about this Norwegian explorer who was the first person to reach both the North Pole and the South Pole.

Yahoo! Kids: Countries—Norway
http://kids.yahoo.com/directory/Around-the-World/Countries/Norway
See color photos of Norway.

INDEX